Belonging to :

FAMILY
Coloring Funny

FAMILY
Coloring Funny

FAMILY
Coloring Funny

FAMILY
Coloring Funny

FAMILY
Coloring Funny

FAMILY
Coloring Funny

FAMILY
Coloring Funny

FAMILY
Coloring Funny

FAMILY
Coloring Funny

FAMILY
Coloring Funny

FAMILY
Coloring Funny

FAMILY
Coloring Funny

FAMILY
Coloring Funny

FAMILY
Coloring Funny

FAMILY

Coloring Funny

FAMILY
Coloring Funny

FAMILY
Coloring Funny

FAMILY
Coloring Funny

FAMILY
Coloring Funny

FAMILY
Coloring Funny

FAMILY
Coloring Funny

FAMILY
Coloring Funny

FAMILY
Coloring Funny

FAMILY
Coloring Funny

FAMILY
Coloring Funny

FAMILY
Coloring Funny

FAMILY
Coloring Funny

FAMILY
Coloring Funny

FAMILY
Coloring Funny

FAMILY
Coloring Funny

FAMILY
Coloring Funny

FAMILY
Coloring Funny

FAMILY
Coloring Funny

FAMILY
Coloring Funny

FAMILY
Coloring Funny

FAMILY
Coloring Funny

FAMILY
Coloring Funny

FAMILY
Coloring Funny

FAMILY
Coloring Funny

FAMILY
Coloring Funny

FAMILY
Coloring Funny

FAMILY
Coloring Funny

FAMILY
Coloring Funny

FAMILY
Coloring Funny

FAMILY

Coloring Funny

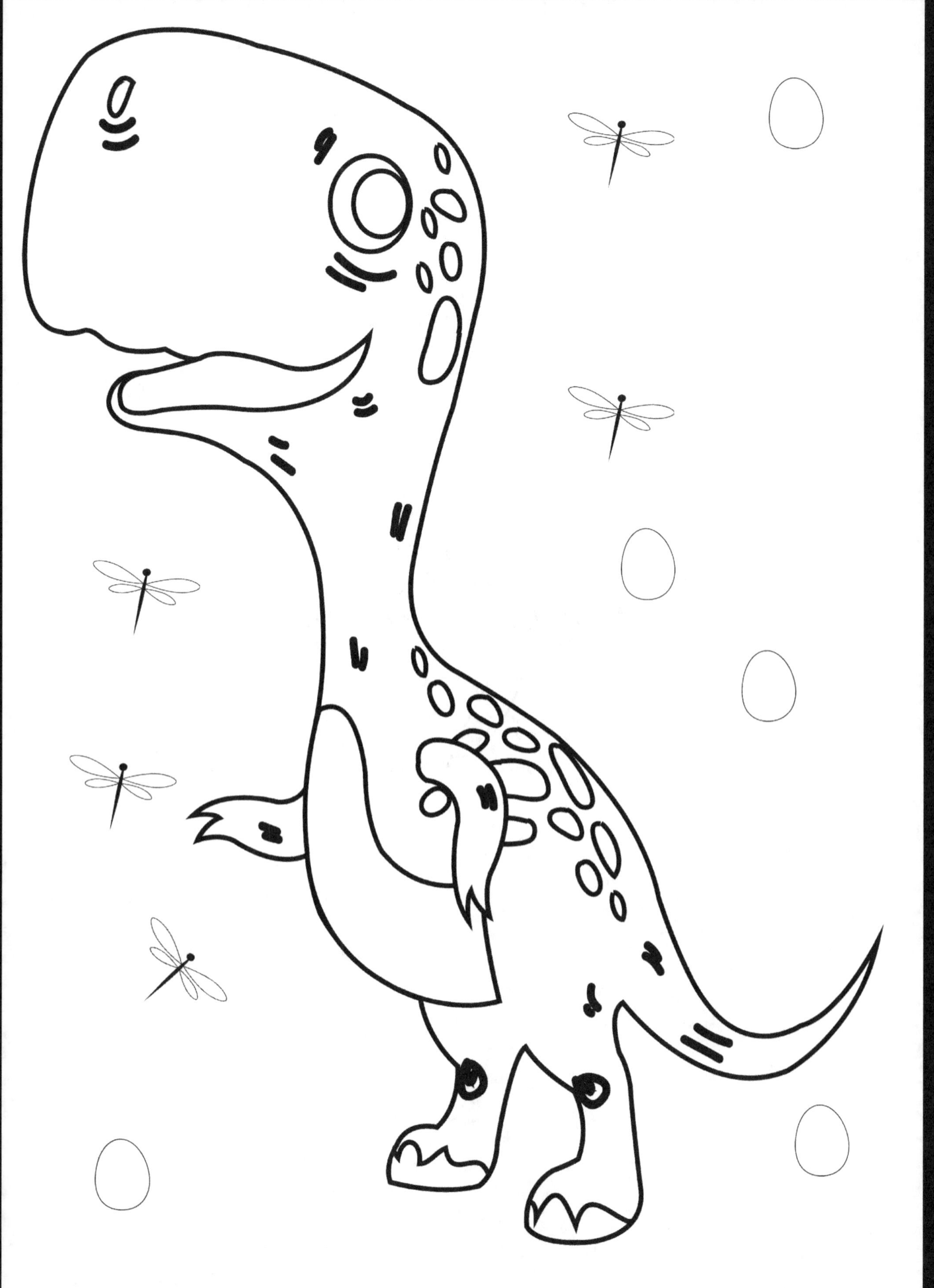

FAMILY
Coloring Funny

FAMILY

Coloring Funny

FAMILY

Coloring Funny

FAMILY
Coloring Funny

FAMILY
Coloring Funny

www.ingramcontent.com/pod-product-compliance
Lightning Source LLC
Chambersburg PA
CBHW081728250726